THE TINY
BOOK OF

Drawings by Mimi Noland

HarperCollinsPublishers

HarperCollins*Publishers*

77-85 Fulham Palace Road,
Hammersmith, London W6 8JB

Published by HarperCollins*Publishers* 1993

9 8 7 6 5 4 3 2 1

Prevlously published in Great Britain by Fontana 1992
Reprinted twice

Copyright © Kathleen Keating 1993
Drawings by Mimi Noland copyright © CompCare Publishers 1987

Published by arrangement with CompCare Publishers

The Author asserts the moral right to
be identified as the author of this work.

ISBN 0 00 637848 X

. . . because we are all holding
each other through a dance of
joy and love.

I embrace with honour
My daughter, Ann Maureen Keating,
and all those at her special place of
learning for the developmentally
disabled, St Vincent School in Santa
Barbara, California
and my son, Matthew Roy Keating
I embrace with gratitude
Golda Clendenin, who inspired me
My friends and colleagues at
Woodview-Calabasas Hospital, who
supported me
Esalen Institute for
teaching me
David Gorton for believing
in me

hug (hug) v.t. hugged,
hugging, hugs.

1. to clasp or hold closely,
especially in one's arms;
embrace or enfold, as in
affection

2. to cherish, hold fast

3.to keep very close to
hug n.
An affectionate embrace.
(From Scandinavian, akin to
old Norse hugga, to comfort,
console.)
hug therapy

The practice of administering hugs for the purpose of curing or healing, or of preserving health.
Treatment of disease through the simple, physical means of hugging.

About hugging and huggers

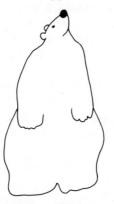

Theory

Touch is not only nice. It's needed. Scientific research supports the theory that stimulation by touch is absolutely necessary for our physical as well as our emotional well-being.

Therapeutic touch, recognised as an essential tool for healing, is now part of nurses' training in several large

A hug makes you feel good
all day.

medical centres. Touch is used to help relieve pain and depression and anxiety, to bolster patients' will to live, to help premature babies — who have been deprived of touch in their incubators — grow and thrive.

Various experiments have shown that touch can:

Make us feel better about ourselves and our surroundings;

Have a positive effect on children's language development and IQ;

Cause measurable physiological changes in the toucher and the touched.

We are just beginning to understand the power of touch.

While there are many forms of touching, we propose that hugging is a very special one that contributes in a major way to healing and health.

Rationale
HUGGING

Feels good

Dispels loneliness

Overcomes fears

Opens doors to feelings

Builds self-esteem ('Wow! *She*
actually wants to hug *me*!')

Fosters altruism ('I can't
believe it, but I actually *want*
to hug that old son-of-a-gun!')

Slows down ageing; huggers
stay younger longer

Helps curb appetite; we eat
less when we are nourished by
hugs — and when our arms are
busy wrapped around others

HUGGING ALSO

Eases tension

Fights insomnia

Keeps arm and shoulder
muscles in condition

Provides stretching exercise if
you are short

Provides stooping exercise if
you are tall

Offers a wholesome alternative
to promiscuity

Offers a healthy, safe alternative to alcohol and other drug abuse (*better hugs than drugs!*)

Affirms physical being

Is democratic; anyone is eligible for a hug

Is ecologically sound, does not upset the environment

Is energy-efficient, saves heat

Is portable

Requires no special equipment

Demands no special setting;
any place from a doorstep to
an executive conference room,
from a church parlour to a
football field, is a fine place
for a hug!

Makes happy days happier

Makes impossible days
possible

Imparts feelings of belonging

Fills up empty places in our
lives

Keeps on working to dispense
benefits even after the hug's
release

Besides, hugging prevents war.

Qualifications

The qualifications for being a
Hug Therapist and being a
client are the same; just being.

Therapeutic hugging is a
mutually healing process. In
fact, hugger and hugged play
interchangeable roles. As a
Hug Therapist, you are open to
the child within you who needs
love, safety, support, caring,
and play, and you are reaching

out to the same needs in the other.

A Hug Therapist does not blame or judge. But he or she does recognise that many of us, in our standoffish society, have not learned to ask for the emotional support we need. If love or support — or play — has been skimpy since childhood, we may feel wounded. If the twistings of growing up have left us with low self-esteem, we may feel unlovable — unhuggable.

Hug Therapists can't solve all these problems, but they can respect the struggles and offer understanding, laughter, gentle words, and an abundance of hugs.

Hug Therapy is not just for the lonely or hurting ones. Hug Therapy can make the healthy healthier, the happy happier, and the most secure among us feel even more so.

Hugging is for everybody.

Anyone can be a Hug Therapist. But if you master the Types of Hugs and the Advanced Techniques presented in this book, you will develop further skills and confidence in your natural ability to share wonderful hugs.

Ethics and rules of conduct

When you are a truly professional Hug Therapist, you take full responsibility for what you say or do. Therefore the hugs you share must be thoughtful, respectful, and care-filled.

These are understood rules of conduct for Hug Therapists:

1. *Since Hug Therapy is always nonsexual, hug*

accordingly. Be sure that the hugs you dispense are compassionate, not passionate. A caring, comforting, or playful hug is different from a lover's embrace. We usually recognise the difference.

No.

If you started out offering or wanting a supportive hug, and it has taken on overtones of greater physical intimacy, just recentre your feelings and thoughts on the original purpose of the hug — to give mutual support.

If you are clear about the kind of hug you are giving, the other hugger most likely will respond in kind. If not, you may want to have a talk about the importance of just-friendly hugs in your relationship.

Yes.

2. *Be certain you have permission before giving a hug.* Often permission to hug is implicit in a relationship. Your sweetheart or a close friend probably will welcome hugs almost any time. However, you still need to respect the other's need for privacy and space.

Sometimes you will receive nonverbal permission from someone who wants a hug, and you respond spontaneously. Or pave the way to hugging with a simple comment like, 'I would like to give you a hug.' Respect the other's verbal and nonverbal messages. Most of the time you will be aware of what is needed and acceptable.

If you misread someone who did not find a hug comfortable, don't be concerned. For some, hugging is very hard; sometimes a sturdy trust must be built before they feel safe enough to hug. Although we Hug Therapists believe the gift

of touch to be extremely
important, the gift of
acceptance is just as
important!

Ask first.

3. *Also be sure to ask permission when you need a hug.* Hug Therapists are not only dispensers of hugs but recipients too. Huggers must sometimes be huggees. Hugging-for-health is a practice of sharing, rather than of just giving or just taking.

When you feel the need for a hug, say: 'I would like a hug, if it's all right with you.' Or, 'I could really use a huge hug right now — would you oblige?'

Or, 'How about a hug before I go off to work?' (or to a meeting or a match or an interview or whatever). A post-hug 'thank you' or 'that felt good' is an important validation of the other's support.

May I have this hug?

4. *Be responsible for expressing what you need and the way you want it.* Blaming others because we're not getting what we need from them is a common mistake we make in our relationships. Some are naturally fine-tuned and intuitive about others' needs and comforts. But most of us — especially if we are busy worrying about our own insecurities — need direct, explicit communication.

If we want more hugs, fewer hugs, ten-second hugs, or two-minute-over-easy hugs — any kind of hug that may be different from what we're getting — we need to say so. Then we have to be willing to compromise as well as to realise that we won't

always get exactly what we
want when we want it.

For some, hugging is very hard.

Contraindications

While Hug Therapists are
convinced that hugging is for
everyone, a few doubters have
trouble accepting Hug Therapy.
They believe, erroneously, that
the sole purpose of a hug is to
build a relationship of physical
intimacy.

A physically intimate embrace
can be beautiful too, but it
meets a different level of

need. This kind of embrace will never replace a good old therapeutic hug! Even intimate partners need bundles of ordinary hugs too.

To keep little ones from acquiring this narrow view of hugs, hug them often — affectionately, supportively, playfully, and tenderly. Let them see parents and other adults hugging in these ways. Otherwise they may grow up believing that hugs are for lovers only, and that in order to be hugged — and huggable — one must be physically attracted to the other hugger.

A Hug Therapist makes every effort to share the broader understanding of touch and hugging and the faith that a day filled with hugs can bring untold satisfaction and serenity.

Fees

Hug Therapy is not free. The
cost is the strength it requires
to be vulnerable. The fee for
hugging is the risk that our
hugs will be rebuffed or
misinterpreted.

When we are very young we
are naturally open. We want
to give love and touch as much
as we want to get love and be
touched. If we're deprived of

love and touch, we become
unwilling to pay the fee of
vulnerability. Love held back
can turn to pain.

Hug Therapists can help ease
this pain. When we risk our
hugs, we affirm our wonderful
ability to share. As we reach
out and touch others, we are
free to discover the
compassion — along with the
capacity for joy — that exists
in all of us. As we become
more spontaneous huggers and

find such inner riches, the fees
seem relatively small.

Thank goodness we have our
softer sides.

Types of hugs

Bear hug

In the traditional bear hug
(named for members of the
family Ursidae, who do it
best), one hugger usually is
taller and broader than the
other, but this is not necessary
to sustain the emotional
quality of bear-hugging. The
taller hugger may stand
straight or slightly curved over
the shorter one, arms wrapped
firmly around the other's

shoulders. The shorter of the pair stands straight with head against the taller hugger's shoulder or chest, arms wrapped — also firmly! — around whatever area between waist and chest that they will reach. Bodies are touching in a powerful, strong squeeze that can last five to ten seconds or more.

We suggest you use skill and forbearance in making the hug firm rather than breathless.

Always be considerate of your partner, no matter what style of hug you are sharing.

The feeling during a bear hug is warm, supportive, and secure.

Bear hugs are for:

Those who share a common feeling or a common cause.

Parents and offspring. Both need lots of reassuring bear hugs.

Grandparents and grand

off-spring. Don't leave
grandparents out of family
bear hugs.

Friends (this includes marrieds and lovers, who hopefully are friends too).

Anyone who wants to say, wordlessly, 'You're terrific!' Or, 'I'm your friend; you can count on me.' Or, 'I share whatever pain or joy you're feeling.'

What can a bear hug say for you?

The A-frame hug

Stand facing each other, wrapping arms around shoulders, sides of heads pressed together and bodies leaning forward and not touching at all below shoulder level. There. You have an A-frame hug. The length of time spent in the A formation is usually brief, since this is often a 'hello' or 'goodbye' hug.

The underlying feeling may be one of polite caring or detached warmth.

The A-frame hug is most appropriate for new acquaintances or professional colleagues, or in situations that require a degree of formality. Because it is relatively nonthreatening, it is comfortable for shy or unpractised huggers.

This is a classic hug and should not be discounted

because of its formal quality. It has broad application and is therefore beneficial to a wide range of huggers.

An A-frame hug is particularly apt for:

A great-aunt whom you haven't seen since you were a toddler.

Your spouse's employer's husband.

Your former academic adviser.

A new daughter-in-law.

Who else?

Like this.

Cheek hug

The cheek hug is a very
tender, gentle hug that often
has a spiritual quality. It can
be experienced comfortably
sitting down, standing up, or
even with one sitting and one
standing, as full body contact
is not necessary.

If you are both seated, turn
comfortably towards each other
and press the sides of your

faces together cheek to cheek. One hand may be on the other's back and the other supporting the back of the head to counteract the pressure of your cheek. Breathe slowly and deeply. Within a few seconds you will feel very relaxed. The cheek hug often stirs deep feelings of kindness, especially when participants are close friends.

A cheek hug is a tasteful way to:

Greet an elderly friend or a relative who is seated.

Say a wordless 'I'm sorry' about a friend's disappointment.

Share a friend's joy at a happy occasion, like a wedding or graduation. (This is a considerate hug for congratulating the principals in reception lines, since it does

not tangle wedding veils or
crush boutonniéres.)

*At what times would you
proffer a cheek hug?*

It often has a spiritual quality.

Sandwich hug

The sandwich hug is a lesser known variety, but once you experience its warmth and security, you'll want to share this one often.

This is a hug for three. Two face each other with the third in the middle facing either one of the others. Each of the two on the outside reaches towards the waist area of the other and hugs. The one in the centre wraps arms around the waist of the facing hugger. As an option, the outside pair may hug around the shoulders and all three snuggle heads together. The bodies are touching cosily.

The sandwich hug gives the one in the middle an especially secure feeling, which is helpful if she or he is going through a difficult time and needs extra support.

The sandwich hug is handy for:

Three good friends.

A couple wishing to comfort someone.

Two parents and a child. The child may be very young, grown up, or any place between.

Make your own sandwich.

Grabber-squeezer hug

The grabber-squeezer hug
holds the record for brevity.
One hugger runs up to and
throws arms about another,
gives a fast squeeze before
letting go, then dashes off.
The one so hugged must be
alert in giving a squeeze in
return, in order to receive
maximum benefit from this hug.

In a variation of the grabber-squeezer, choreographically more difficult, both run towards each other and give a quick, simultaneous squeeze. Safety note: Avoid a collision course. The full-force crash of two bodies who have hurtled together or the knocking of two heads may negate some of the good feelings!

Feelings vary with the situation, but often the grabber-squeezer is accompanied by a sense of affectionate distraction because one or both of the huggers are rushed. If the huggee is not expecting it, there also may be a feeling of surprise.

Grab-and-squeeze hugging is a practical way to work in a lot of fast hugging when you're on a tight schedule. For more effective stress management, also include a liberal sprinkling of hugs that are gentler and last longer.

Use the grabber-squeezer:
In the workshop or the kitchen.
To wish someone luck before a
performance.

As a silent translation of the words 'I like you a lot, but I'm in a terrible hurry!'

How can the grabber-squeezer fit into your life?

There also may be a feeling of surprise.

Group hug

The group hug is a very popular hug for good friends sharing in an activity or project. As Hug Therapists, we would like the group hug to be better known and more often applied, just because it feels so good.

The group forms a circle — its members standing as close together as possible, arms

around shoulders or waists —
and squeezes. In a variation,
group hug participants, holding
each other as above, move in
towards the centre, shrinking
the circle. They huddle
together for several moments,
then back up and break apart
with a cheer or sigh or a quick,
parting squeeze.

Besides good feelings of
support, security, and
affection, group hugs often
impart a sense of unity and

universal belonging.

Group hugs are good for:

Growth groups.

Support groups.

Classmates, teammates.

Hardworking committees.

Any bunch you like.

When would your group
welcome a hug like this?

A group hug often imparts a
sense of universal belonging.

Side-to-side hug

The side-to-side hug, or the lateral squeeze, is a great hug to get and give while walking along together. As you stroll side by side with an arm around the other's waist or over the shoulder, once in a while give a generous squeeze.
This is also a merry and playful hug for those moments

when you are standing in line
with a friend. It makes
queuing up a pleasure!

The side-to-side hug provides
a joyful moment while:

Walking to a bus.

On a hike or an archaeological
dig.

Waiting to get into a Saturday
night movie or to register for
next term's classes.

When could you use a side-to-side hug?

Back-to-front hug

In the back-to-front hug (also known as the waist-grabber), the hugger approaches the other from the back, folds arms around his or her waist and gives a gentle hug.

The back-to-front waist-grabber is the perfect hug to give someone who is peeling potatoes, scrubbing pans over a kitchen sink, or otherwise engaged in some routine stand-up chore. A somewhat old-fashioned hug, this was practised more extensively before the invention of the automatic dishwasher. But most of the time a waist-grabber is still welcome as a brief, playful gesture. The feeling behind it is happy and supportive.*

*Even more supportive would be the back-to-front hug followed by the picking up of a teatowel and applying it to the pans.

Back-to-front hugs are for:

Househusbands, housewives, and other live-ins.

Co-workers on an assembly line.

Friends whose occupations require that they face mostly in one direction — like raspberry-pickers or mail-sorters.

Do you know someone who would appreciate a waist-grabber?

Custom-tailored hug

The most effective hug for you
is the hug that feels right,
considering the setting, the
situation, the one you are with,
and what you personally need
from the hug (affection,
strength and support,
reaffirmation of a bond of
friendship, relaxation, or any
other good feeling that a hug
can bring.)

Sometimes a custom-tailored hug is called for, as in the case of an extra-tall hugger and a very short huggee (or vice versa). Or when the hug, in order to please both parties equally, has to include a jealous pet or a favourite toy too.

Be creative. True Hug Therapists do not let circumstances stand in their way.

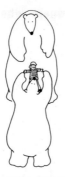

A custom-tailored hug may have
to include a favourite toy.

Hugs: where, when, why

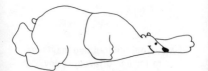

Environments

A place of beauty enhances
the experience of hugging.
Whatever setting you consider
beautiful — a peaceful country
path on a warm, clear day or a
scrap of green park that opens
a city to the sky — can make
the hug you share with a friend
even more special.

However, if the setting seems
shabby or bleak, it can be

totally transformed just because you are sharing a hug.

Any place is the right place for hugging when the heart is open.

A hug transforms a bleak setting . . .

. . . into a lovely place.

Time of the day

Some are morning,
up-and-at-'em huggers.
Some are evening, thank-
heaven-the-day-is-over
huggers. Some like to hug
at high noon on lunch
hours or at teatime. Although
routine hugs are fine,
sometimes the most
appreciated hugs happen
spontaneously at unexpected
moments.

Friendship

Compassion

The feelings that bring on a hug — affection, sympathy, caring, just plain joy — can happen at any time of day. So can hug situations, like bumping into an old school friend at an airport. True Hug

Joy

Feelings that bring on a hug . . .

Therapists will entertain the
idea of a hug at any time. And
hugs scattered through the day
will help to maintain a sense of
well-being, belonging, and
self-esteem.

. . . can happen any time.

Advanced techniques

Visualisation

Visualisation is a powerful technique for learning and change. One way we learn is through repeated imprintings on our minds — not only of what we actually view in the world around us, but also of pictures we see in our imaginations. Imagined pictures, which can affect us as strongly as reality, sometimes even set off physical responses.

Think about slicing a juicy
lemon and squeezing the tart
juice into your mouth. Your
mouth waters at the very
thought. You may detect a
sour taste too. You have the
sensation of sucking a lemon
even though there's no real
lemon anywhere in sight.

Now try visualising yourself
hugging somebody. Let this
imagined hug register in your
mind as a nourishing
experience. A mind picture

like this can teach you to see yourself as someone who is at ease giving and getting warm, caring hugs.

In guided imagery, you plan or guide the direction you'd like your imagination to take. So let's say you would like to be comfortable greeting a friend with a heart-centred hug. Sit in a comfortable, quiet place and close your eyes. Breathe slowly and deeply four or five

An imagined hug is a nourishing
experience.

times and let your body relax totally. Imagine yourself walking along and meeting a good friend. Picture the two of you saying hello by putting your arms around each other and sharing a heart-centred hug.

Keep the picture in your mind as you sense good feelings of affection and warmth. It is important to put the imagined picture and the feelings together.

Or use guided imagery when
you are feeling the need for
support after a stressful day.
Visualise a favourite friend
who is also a good hugger
giving you a very fond and
supportive hug. Imagine that
friend holding you and offering
you reassurance and love.
Keep the picture and the
feelings in your mind for as
long as you need comfort.

Zen hugging

You can use any type of hug
for Zen hugging. Our
favourites are the cheek-to-
cheek hug or the heart-centred
hug. A very connected touch
— a feet-to-feet and hands-to-
hands touch, for instance —
will do fine too.

Your eyes may be open or
closed. Focus on your
breathing, and allow it to

become even and deep. You
will begin to feel yourself
relaxing. You are centred in
the present moment. Let go of
all thinking. All that is present
is the experience of your
senses.

You are aware of the warmth
you are sharing, of your breath
moving in and out, of the touch
of the other person, of the air
on your skin. Relax. Be
suspended in time. The longer

you are able to relax in the
present moment, the deeper
will be your experience of the
hug or the touching.

Peace.

You are centred in the present
moment.

Institute of hug therapy

We believe more must be done
to break down the cultural and
emotional barriers that prevent
us from experiencing the
healthy nourishment of
touching and hugging. The
establishment of the Institute
of Hug Therapy is our
whimsical, but earnest,
contribution to that effort.

Becoming a member of the
Institute of Hug Therapy is

easy. Just believe in the power of hugging! Wear the title of Hug Therapist proudly. Tell others about hugging for health. Spread the pro-hug philosophy wherever you go.

Hugging should not be something you do once in a while, at family reunions or birthdays or when one of your teammates makes a goal. Our hope is that hugging will become commonplace, without detracting from the

specialness of each separate
hug.

Hug often. Hug well.